Worry

by Jan

LONGMAN

On Monday morning the door of Herman's cage was open and Herman had gone. After assembly Mrs Collier held a public enquiry.

"Who was the last person to touch the cage on Friday?" she said, looking round at the class.

The class looked back.

"It wasn't me," Sophie said.

"I know it wasn't you,"
Mrs Collier said, impatiently.
"You weren't here."

CRAFT CUPBOARD
It wasn't me.

Sophie was the Herman Monitor, but she had been at home with a cold on Friday. She was still pink around the nose and snuffling slightly, rather like Herman himself.

Ciaran looked away from Mrs Collier and studied his knees. He had a nasty feeling that he had been the last person to touch the guinea-pig's cage, but he was sure that he had fastened it. He was like Mum, everyone said so. Mum always went back twice to make sure that she had switched off the iron or turned out the gas.

Perhaps somebody else had come back into the room after they had all left, and taken Herman out for a last cuddle. Perhaps Herman had let himself out. He was not very intelligent, even for a guinea-pig, but he might have been keeping an eye on the lock, watching to see how it worked, and when the room was empty he had put his little leathery paw between the bars and lifted the catch.

"He couldn't have let himself out," Mrs Collier said, as if she knew what Ciaran was thinking. "Someone isn't telling the truth."

"Maybe thieves broke in and stole him," Kershid suggested. "Like climbed on the wheelie bins, over the roof ..."

"I don't think so," Mrs Collier said. "If anyone had gone to all that trouble, they'd have taken the computers, not Herman."

No one admitted to leaving the cage open. Mrs Collier gave up, and the class took out books for silent reading. It was Ciaran's favourite time of the day. His seat was close to the shelf where Herman lived, and during the silence he would listen to the small, comfortable sounds of Herman turning circles in his straw, nibbling stalks, snuffling to himself. Today the silence was terribly silent.

Suppose it *was* his fault that Herman had gone. He could not concentrate on the words in front of him. From his work tray he took his rough jotter and opened it at the back, where he kept The List.

The List had begun weeks ago when he borrowed the spare back-door keys without asking, because he could not find his own. Then he lost them. He wrote KEYS on the inside cover of the book to remind him to look for them, which was not really necessary because he never stopped thinking about them.

By the time he had found them both and crossed out KEYS, he had written PE KIT underneath, because he had left his own at home and borrowed Hamid's from 5GH and then forgot where he had put it.

After that, he had added MUM'S MONEY because he was saving up to buy her a birthday present and never seemed to get past 70p.

The list was growing longer. Occasionally something would get crossed off, but there was always another worry to add. One thing never got crossed off. It was half-way down the cover and it would not go away. SATS.

If he thought about SATS, he could see it, a squat lurking thing with a long snappy beak full of teeth, that was lying in wait for him.

It would not get him yet, there was more than a year to go, but SATS got everybody in the end.

The last item on The List was SPEECH MARKS. Speech marks were part of the SATS trap, but they had a line to themselves because, of all the things he was supposed to know, they were the ones he always forgot.

Under SPEECH MARKS he wrote HERMAN'S CAGE, and then, BIKE PUMP. He had forgotten about the pump. It must be lying in a gutter somewhere. He had borrowed Lena's bike to go to the shop, and when he came back the pump was no longer on the bike. Lena was going to beat him up about that.

Mum often told Lena that she should not beat up her brother, but Lena would do it anyway if he did not find the pump.

Silent reading time was over and he had not read a word.

Beware of big Sister!

After break it was time for Art. They were making posters for Book Week and Ciaran had chosen *The Lion, the Witch and the Wardrobe* for his poster. He had never read it, but he liked doing lions. He had plans for a flowing mane with bits of yellow string and he thought he could have a wardrobe with a real door that opened on hinges made of sticky tape.

Mrs Collier let him look in the craft cupboard for string, and while he was in there, he heard a familiar sound which was strange because it was in an unfamiliar place. It was

Red
Blue
Plasticine Bits
Yellow
Brown

coming from right down on the floor where the tissue paper was kept. Something was moving about.

He went down on hands and knees and looked under the lowest shelf. There was Herman, in a cosy nest that he had made for himself out of paper.

"Come on out," Ciaran said, and Herman allowed himself to be lifted away from his nest. Ciaran felt Herman's small hurried heart-beat as he cradled him against his shirt, and backed out of the cupboard.

"Look what I found," he said.

There was a small burst of applause, and everyone left their places to make sure that it really was Herman and that he was quite safe.

"Sit down all of you," Mrs Collier said. "Ciaran, put him back in his cage, and *make sure the door's shut this time.*"

Ciaran lowered Herman into his straw and pushed the clasp down firmly. Now that Herman was found, he could allow himself to remember Friday afternoon, how he had been giving Herman a piece of carrot when Mrs Collier had told them to hurry up and go to the hall for hymn practice.

Perhaps Herman's escape had been his fault, but it was all over now and he could stop worrying. He went back to his table, took out the rough jotter and put a line through HERMAN'S CAGE.

"What's that?" Sophie said. Ciaran did not much like sitting next to Sophie. There was nothing wrong with Sophie herself, but she was so *tidy*. Her pencil case was never full of old sweet wrappers and covered in felt-tip scribbles. Her pens never leaked. Her pencils were always sharpened.

"Mind your own business," Ciaran said, and put his arm around the book, but it was too late. Sophie had leaned across to look at The List.

"Keys, bike pump, PE kit, Mum's money, Herman's cage?" she said, reading from the back cover. "Is that a list of lost things?"

"I said mind your own business," Ciaran said.

"SATS?" Sophie said. "How can you lose SATS?"

"It isn't lost things," Ciaran growled. "It's just things I'm worried about."

"Why are you worried about SATS? It isn't for months and months and months."

"Well, even if it was years and years and years and years, it's still going to happen, isn't it? I've still got to pass it."

"You don't pass SATS," Sophie argued. "They're only tests. You just have to do them. There's nothing to worry about."

"If we didn't have to worry we wouldn't have to do them," Ciaran said. "If they didn't matter there wouldn't be any, would there?"

"I'm not worried," Sophie said.

"Well, you wouldn't be, would you? You always get everything right.

Even speech marks."

"It's not that," Sophie said. She unzipped her pencil case and took out a little cloth bag that was stowed right at the end of it. She opened the bag and tipped something out on to the table. "These are my trouble dolls."

The trouble dolls were tiny, two or three centimetres high, and covered with coloured cotton. There were six of them, all different.

“What are they for?”

“They’re special, specially made for troubles. They come from Guatemala – that’s in South America. You tell them your worries at night time and put them back in the bag, and they take care of the worries during the night. You can only give them one worry each.”

Kershid was leaning over on the other side. “Do they work?”

“Yes, my auntie gave them to me.”

“Your auntie’s been to South America?”

"No, she got them in Luton."

Kershid picked up a doll and examined it. "Could I borrow one?"

"I don't think they work for other people," Sophie said, nervously. "I'm not being mean, or anything." Kershid had big hands and the doll looked even tinier. "What are you worried about?"

"Arabic," Kershid said, gloomily. "I have to read the Koran in Arabic and I keep forgetting it." He put the doll back with the others. "I don't suppose we're meant to use things like this, anyway. It's a whatsit, a superstition."

"Don't care if it is," Sophie said.

She tenderly tucked the dolls into the bag. “They look after my worries.”

Ciaran went back to the cupboard, to fetch his string. On the next shelf along were the ice cream tubs that still said Raspberry Ripple and Chocolate Chip on the lids, but now contained Plasticine. Mrs Collier kept a different colour in each tub, but Tutti-frutti had the purplish lumps that were all the colours mixed together. He opened the lid and took out a piece, twiddling it in his fingers until it

grew a head, and a long flopping tail, a sort of dinosaur monster.

He wasn't going to fool around with trouble dolls, which were babyish and girlie, but why not make a trouble monster? Dinosaur could be the bike-pump worry. He put it on the shelf and took another piece. This one was coming out lumpy. It had bits of grit in it. Speech marks, he thought.

Mrs Collier looked into the cupboard.

"Ciaran, have you found that string yet?"

"Yes, Miss." He grabbed a handful of string and, at the same time, a handful of Plasticine.

He took them back to the table and, while Mrs Collier looked his way, he cut the string into six-centimetre lengths for the lion's mane and stuck it on to his poster. When she looked at anyone else he worked on his monsters. Each time he finished one he put it into his work tray to harden off as it cooled down. By the end of the morning he had a monster for each worry, except for SATS. SATS needed something special.

When it was time to clear up for lunch he took the rest of the string back to the craft cupboard and opened the Banana Split tub. Mrs Collier kept the yellow Plasticine in there. He did not know why, but SATS sounded yellow, the way that September sounded light brown and Wednesday tasted of bleach. He put the yellow Plasticine in his pocket and went to lunch.

When he came back the trouble monsters were nice and firm. It was a wet play day and he sat in the corner of the hall behind the

vaulting horse and kneaded the lump of yellow Plasticine until it was as soft as putty. Then he moulded it into a fat greedy body and pulled at one end until he had a head that tapered off into a long beak. He laid the SATS monster on the cold sweaty radiator to get hard. By the end of lunch break, SATS was leathery enough for Ciaran to make fangs with a pencil point, all along the beak.

Somehow, having the trouble monsters where he could see them, made the troubles less threatening than they seemed when written down in The List. He found the bicycle pump next morning. It had fallen off even before he got out of the gate, and

was lying hidden among the rhubarb leaves by the path. He went indoors and waved it at Lena, who snatched it away in disappointment because she had been looking forward to beating him up.

At school he pulled out his work tray from under the table and looked at the trouble monsters. He no longer needed bike-pump monster, so he rolled it up and stuck it to SATS like a large wart.

Next morning Mrs Collier moved a stack of magazines from beside

Herman's cage and underneath, squashed flat, was the PE kit that he had borrowed from Hamid. Two days later, Mr Bryant next door gave him £3 for helping to clear rubbish from his allotment, and when he added it to his pocket money, he had enough for the birthday present.

Gradually the trouble monsters were getting fewer and fewer. Each time he got rid of a worry he rolled its monster into a ball and stuck it to SATS. SATS was not going to go away, and by now it was an

extremely nasty monster, covered in warts and boils. People often asked to look at SATS because it was so very unpleasant.

One day Mrs Collier came out of the craft cupboard and said, “What has happened to all the Plasticine?”

No one said anything.

Mrs Collier stood at her desk, looking serious. “Someone has been stealing the Plasticine,” she said. “At first I thought I was imagining it, but I had a look just now and all the yellow Plasticine has gone. Who took it?”

Ciaran knew that he would have to own up or there would be another trouble monster in his tray. He put up his hand.

"I did, Miss."

"*All* of it?" Mrs Collier said.

"No, just some." He pulled out his tray and took out SATS. SATS was four times the size it had been to start with.

"What on earth is that?" Mrs Collier said.

"It's my SATS monster," Ciaran said.

"Your *what*?"

“Oh, Miss,” Sophie said, “I showed him my trouble dolls and he’s made trouble monsters.”

“I see,” Mrs Collier said. “But that doesn’t account for several kilograms of Plasticine going missing. Where’s the rest, Ciaran?”

He did not have to answer. Everyone in the class was pulling out trays. Plasticine monsters appeared on each table. Everyone had a different idea of what SATS looked like, but they were all horrible, squat and lumpy.

"Are these all SATS monsters?" Mrs Collier said.

Everyone nodded.

"What's the idea?"

"It's like my trouble dolls," Sophie said. She explained how they worked.

"Yes," Mrs Collier said. "I've seen Sophie's dolls. They're very small. You SATS monsters have used up almost all the Plasticine in the class. Are you really so worried about SATS?"

Everyone nodded again.

"What about my Plasticine? I'll tell you what, let's make one huge economy-size SATS monster and put it where we can see it. It'll be a sort of public worry."

They made the SATS monster out of chicken wire with strips of newspaper pasted round it. It had a long beak

GL
GL

with dozens of teeth, cruel claws, wings, feathers and lots of warts. Kershid's dad worked for the electricity company and he brought in some co-axial cable so that SATS could grow a long multi-coloured tail. When it was finished, they hung it from the ceiling above Herman's cage.

Mr Harvey, from 5GH, had his classroom on the other side of the playground. When he saw SATS hanging from the ceiling and turning gently in the warm air, he came across to investigate.

“This is our SATS monster,” Mrs Collier explained. “People were worrying secretly about SATS so we made a monster to do our worrying for us, and we keep it where we can see it.”

Mr Harvey laughed. “You’re not thinking about SATS already, are you? They won’t happen for ages. Isn’t it a bit silly to start worrying so soon?”

“It’s all right for you,” Kershid said, “*You* haven’t got anything to worry about.”

"What makes you think that?" Mrs Collier asked.

"Well, you're grown up and you've got a good job," Kershid said.

"Grown-ups have plenty to worry about, Kershid," Mr Harvey said, "even if they have got jobs."

"It's the jobs they worry about," Mrs Collier said. "Our trouble monster is called Inspection."

"What's that?" Ciaran said.

"Inspectors are people who come into school to see if we're doing

You've got a good job.

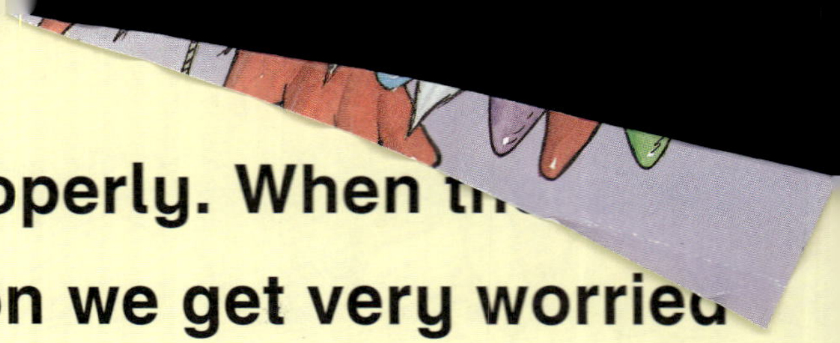

our work properly. When th
an inspection we get very worried
indeed. Perhaps we'd better make
a monster for the staffroom."

"Oh, you needn't bother about
that," Kershid said with an
innocent smile. "We'll sort them
out for you, Miss. We'll tell them
you've teached us proper!"